T0378532

Exploring Chinese Mythology

Don Nardo

ReferencePoint Press

San Diego, CA

About the Author

Classical historian and award-winning author Don Nardo has written numerous acclaimed volumes about ancient civilizations and peoples. They include more than three dozen overviews of the mythologies of the Sumerians, Babylonians, Egyptians, Greeks, Romans, Persians, Celts, Chinese, Aztecs, Native Americans, and others. Nardo, who also composes and arranges orchestral music, lives with his wife, Christine, in Massachusetts.

© 2023 ReferencePoint Press, Inc.
Printed in the United States

For more information, contact:
ReferencePoint Press, Inc.
PO Box 27779
San Diego, CA 92198
www.ReferencePointPress.com

Picture Credits:
Cover: Trend Graphics/Shutterstock.com

 6: Rainer Lesniewski//Shutterstock.com
10: John Astor/Alamy Stock Photo
13: The Print Collector/Alamy Stock Photo
15: Art Collection 2/Alamy Stock Photo
19: Pictures from History/Bridgeman Images
22: zhang jiahan/Alamy Stock Photo
25: Bill Perry/Shutterstock.com

30: ©San Diego Museum of Art/Bequest of Mrs. Cora Timken/Bridgeman Images
32: CPA Media Pte Ltd/Alamy Stock Photo
36: Lebrecht History/Brideman Images
40: Fenny Juiany/Shutterstock.com
43: Pictures from History/Bridgeman Images
44: Jac.Q/Shutterstock.com
48: Erickson Stock/Shutterstock.com
52: ©Archives Charmet/Bridgeman Images
55: ©NPL-DeA Picture Library/Bridgeman Images

Photo Researcher: Olivia Habib

LIBRARY OF CONGRESS CATALOGING-IN-PUBLICATION DATA

Names: Nardo, Don, 1947- author.
Title: Exploring Chinese mythology / by Don Nardo.
Description: San Diego, CA : ReferencePoint Press, Inc., [2022] | Includes bibliographical references and index.
Identifiers: LCCN 2022024755 (print) | LCCN 2022024756 (ebook) | ISBN 9781678204785 (library binding) | ISBN 9781678204792 (ebook)
Subjects: LCSH: Mythology, Chinese.
Classification: LCC BL1803 .N37 2022 (print) | LCC BL1803 (ebook) | DDC 398.20951--dc23/eng20220826
LC record available at https://lccn.loc.gov/2022024755
LC ebook record available at https://lccn.loc.gov/2022024756

CONTENTS

A History Highlighted by Greatness

In its earliest era—thousands of years ago—China was a beautiful, picturesque, almost storybook-like land of rolling hills, deep fragrant forests, and lush river valleys. There was plenty of work, food, and prosperity for all its inhabitants. That idyllic situation changed rather suddenly, however, during the reign of a well-meaning emperor named Yao. Some of his subjects decided that the benefits they enjoyed were not enough, and some of them began to steal from others. That led to bad feelings and bloody fights among various individuals, families, and villages.

Up in the heavenly sphere lying high above the clouds, several of the many gods who controlled nature and the world looked down on the disturbances on the earth's surface. Disappointed and angry, they agreed among themselves that the humans needed to be punished. So the celestial beings caused torrential rains to shower down upon the land. The deluge went on day after day, week after week, until, as one modern account describes it,

the whole of the earth resembled one vast ocean. Those who were fortunate enough to avoid drowning floated on the treacherous waters in search of tall trees or high mountains where they might come to rest. But even if they managed to reach dry land, they were then forced to compete with the fiercest beasts of the earth for food, so that many were mercilessly devoured. Only one god among the deities of the heavens appeared to feel any sympathy for the innocent people suffering such appalling misery on earth. The god's name was Gun.[1]

Indeed, Gun was so concerned for the suffering humans that he attempted to make the floodwaters recede. Seeing this, however, Yan-di, god of fire, lost his temper and slew Gun. At least, Yan-di *thought* he had killed his fellow deity. In actuality, Gun was only unconscious. Moreover, unknown to the other divinities, a child was growing inside Gun's body. That god, Yu, soon emerged into the world in the form of a magnificent gold-colored dragon.

> **Yan-di**
> The Chinese god of fire

> **Yu**
> An early Chinese god who helped save the human race from a great flood

Like his father, Yu desired to save the surviving humans. And to that noble end, the young dragon hastily built a large dam out of rocks and soil, a barrier that succeeded in containing the floodwaters. When the other gods beheld this achievement, they were mightily impressed. So they did not interfere when he flew upward and dispersed the rain clouds, ending the flood. Afterward, Yu asked another powerful god, Ying Long, often called the Dragon King, to help him repair the extensive damage the floods had caused. In response, the surviving humans sang hymns of thanksgiving for their divine saviors.

A Distinctly Harmonious System

Tales of large-scale natural disasters like the great flood that Yu halted contributed to a theme quite prevalent in ancient Chinese mythical lore. Other common themes included the creation of the world and humankind; the adventures of heroes and the villains

This map shows modern China with its many provinces. In ancient times there were only a few such subdivisions, then clustered mainly in the east/central region.

they opposed; lyrical stories of love and lovers; accounts of fierce dragons and other fantastical beasts; and tales of skilled warriors and the battles they fought, to name only a few.

One feature that almost all the Chinese myths have in common is that they reflect the beliefs, customs, and traditions of the distinctive Chinese society that generated them. For many generations, China remained mostly isolated from outside cultural influences. So its myths represent a distinctly Chinese point of view. This is different from the myths of European cultures, which were influenced by peoples around the globe. "Of course," says Chinese-born British scholar Tao Tao Liu Sanders, "there were invaders and conquerors who came to China. But their cultures were always less developed than the Chinese. And they nearly always ended up by being absorbed into Chinese culture themselves."[2]

One notable exception is Buddhism's spread from nearby India into China beginning in the first century CE. That faith was not primarily god centered, like those of the Greeks, the Norse, and later the Christians. Rather, Buddhism is based on the idea that unhappiness is caused by suffering and that suffering can be overcome through compassion, kindness, and consideration toward other people. In China, Buddhist beliefs rapidly blended with already existing Taoist and Confucian concepts, which also, as Sanders points out, "taught a practical social order which enabled people to live in harmony with each other." One might call the combination of these ideas a harmonious belief system. Although a number of supernatural deities dating from China's earliest eras were still recognized over the centuries, they were in a sense secondary to that harmonious belief system. It teaches people, Sanders explains, to live "their lives according to a moral code."[3]

A Strong Sense of Right and Wrong

Thus, whatever themes are explored in the old Chinese myths, they retain a distinctive cultural flavor that is different in certain ways from that of the ancient Greek myths and other European-based mythologies. When Greek heroes fight monsters and human villains, for instance, the emphasis is typically on the bravery and fighting skills of those heroes. When ancient Chinese heroes fight, in comparison, the stories tend to stress those warriors' superior sense of right and wrong. Therefore, in the words of University of Cambridge professor Anne Birrell, "Chinese heroic myths differ from other mythologies in their emphasis on the moral virtue of the warrior hero."[4]

In a way, the Chinese people feel that the ethical qualities of their leading mythical characters mirror or echo the moral code of their long-lived civilization. They believe that several of the heroes and deities in the myths were either real people or at least based on historical figures. In their eyes, therefore, their history is frequently highlighted by great individuals and deeds. And the inspiring examples those characters provide, Birrell states, "reflects the power of myth to affirm and re-enact the sacred history of a nation."[5]

CHAPTER ONE

Pangu, Nuwa, and the World's Creation

To this day no one knows for sure where the original cosmic egg came from. That egg, inhabited by the first divine being, floated by itself in the ether of existence for a very long time. Resting comfortably within that special celestial seed, Pangu (as the being became known) remained fast asleep for eighteen thousand years and then finally woke up and burst out of the egg. For all those years he had been growing, which explains why at the moment he hatched and awakened, he was physically enormous in stature.

Over the centuries Chinese artists have depicted Pangu in many colorful ways. Some pictured him as naked and covered with fur. Others showed him wearing the hairy hide of a bear, and still others gave him a dog's head or a man's head with big horns growing from his huge skull.

Regardless of how he is depicted, the tales of Pangu all make it clear that his actions set the world's history in motion. Disturbed by the fact that nothing existed beyond himself and the cosmic egg's remnants, he became obsessed with the idea of creation. He realized that making things would require tools, and to that end he conjured up the image of an ax in his mind. Almost instantly, that item materialized in his right hand. Using the ax, he broke up the remaining pieces of his birth egg. As he did so, the lightest sections drifted upward to become the sky, and the heaviest parts sank downward to form the earth.

After that, writes University of California, Berkeley scholar Cyril Birch, each day the earth grew thicker and the sky rose higher. Also, Pangu himself grew larger until he was nothing less than gigantic. Birch continues, "Thousands of miles tall he stood, a great pillar separating earth from sky, so that the two might never again come together to dissolve once more into a single chaos. Throughout long ages he stood until the time when he could be sure that earth and sky were fixed and firm in their places. When this time came, Pangu, his task achieved, lay down on earth to rest and died."[6]

Even in death, however, Pangu retained the power to create. Parts of his body transformed the universe. As Chinese scholars Lihui Yang and Deming An tell it:

His breath became the winds and clouds, his voice became the thunder, his left eye became the sun, his right eye became the moon, his four limbs and trunk became the [continents] . . . his blood became the rivers . . . his flesh became fields and soil, his hair and beard became the stars, his skin and body hair became plants, [and] his teeth and bones became various metals and rocks.[7]

Pangu's tale is the most popular Chinese creation story, but it is not the only one. A number of other folk tales about the world's creation emerged in diverse parts of China in ancient times. Some of those myths describe the origins of the original, or primeval, gods as stemming from sudden loud sounds, powerful air currents, or a special variety of mud. Still another version suggests that a strange creature called Hundun predated the universe. In that tale, Hundun had a torso, legs, and wings but no mouth, nose, eyes, navel, or other bodily openings. One day some deities decided to help Hundun by drilling holes for its mouth, eyes, and so forth. After all the holes were drilled, the tale claims, Hundun died, and the known universe grew from its corpse.

The creator of the universe in ancient Chinese mythology holds the celestial cosmic egg. Pangu is said to have burst from the egg after sleeping within it for eighteen thousand years.

A Race of Mortal Worshippers

According to these various myths, the fashioning of the physical universe marked only the initial phase of creation. Human beings and the societies they developed over time had yet to emerge. Accordingly, several additional creation stories evolved in ancient China to account for humanity's origins.

Of those tales, by far the most prevalent and popular is that of the goddess Nuwa and her miraculous exploits. During the many years that Pangu was molding various aspects of the world, individual bursts of energy periodically appeared high up in the sky. They were random and came seemingly out of nowhere. Each of these phantom-like eruptions in space steadily coalesced into a lifeform that was both powerful and immortal. These were the gods who succeeded Pangu and over time established the thousands of complex processes that make up nature.

These early divinities were mightily impressed by what Pangu had wrought. But one of their number—Nuwa—felt that the giant creator being had left out something important. That missing piece, she concluded, was a race of mortal creatures who could both maintain the newly made world and worship the emerging gods. With Pangu already dead, Nuwa took it upon herself to construct those mortal creatures, whom she called human beings. But where would she make them, she wondered, and with what sort of materials? After giving it some thought, she chose

The Five August Emperors

Among the most important and beloved of the many culture heroes recognized in Chinese mythology are five rulers collectively known as the Five August Emperors. The first, Huang-di, the so-called Yellow Emperor, was said to have ruled China from 2697 to 2597 BCE. He is credited with the invention of mathematics and astronomy, as well as the system of notes that musicians read and play. The second August Emperor, Zhuanxu, purportedly reigned from 2514 to 2436 BCE. He supposedly introduced several religious reforms, including meeting with the gods and convincing them to visit the earth only under urgent circumstances. Next came Ku, said to have ruled from 2436 to 2366 BCE. Ku's main claims to fame were the enthusiastic promotion of music and the invention of many new musical instruments. Legends claim that the fourth August Emperor, Yao, ruled from 2358 to 2258 BCE. A skilled politician, Yao united many large and powerful families, thereby promoting peace and prosperity. The fifth and last August Emperor, the brilliant statesman Shun, supposedly reigned from 2258 to 2195 BCE. He inspired loyalty and patriotism among the Chinese people by persuading them to work together with the aim of creating a better society.

China's Yellow River valley as the spot and settled on the rich soil lining that waterway's banks as her building material. Delicately molding each little body from the mud, she fashioned several hundred humans. Soon, however, she realized that it would take her too long to make an entire race of beings this way; so she devised a faster method. According to Yang and An, "She took a cord [made of sugar cane] and pulled it through the mud, then lifted the cord and shook it. All of the sludge that fell down from the cord became men and women. One version of the myth explains that rich and noble people were those made by Nuwa's hands, whereas poor and lowly people were those made by Nuwa dragging the cord through the mud."[8]

Nuwa to the Rescue

One thing that Nuwa noticed was that, unlike herself and the other gods, the little beings she had created grew old and died. That meant they had to be able to reproduce themselves from time to time. "To solve this problem," Birch explains, "Nuwa brought together man and woman and taught them the ways of marriage. Now they could create for themselves their own sons and daughters, and these in turn could continue to people the earth throughout time."[9]

As it turned out, Nuwa not only created the human race and introduced the institution of marriage but also saved her creations from an early extinction. A mere two or three generations after humanity's appearance, the fire deity Yan-di became extremely annoyed with the god of fresh water, Gong-gong. Exactly why Yan-di was so upset is a bit of knowledge that has been lost in the mists of time. It may have been because Gong-gong often marshaled rainstorms to douse the forest fires that Yan-di ignited.

Whatever the reason for the dispute, Gong-gong eventually lost the argument and in a fit of despair banged his head against a mountaintop that Pangu had earlier erected to help hold up the heavens. The peak was so badly damaged that a section of the sky

The goddess Nuwa is described as having a serpent's body and human head. She created the human race and the concept of marriage.

collapsed. Not only did the crash kill many people, it also caused a chain reaction of earthquakes and other natural disasters that threatened to destroy all of humankind, along with most animals.

Having fashioned the humans only a few years before, Nuwa could not bear the thought of their sudden eradication and became determined to save them. Diving downward from the heavens, she grabbed hold of the carcass of a monstrous turtle that had recently died. Swiftly, she removed its legs and employed them like pillars to hold up the portions of the sky that were still unstable. Next she scooped up masses of boulders and hastily built a giant fire pit, in which she melted the boulders down into a glue-like substance. With that she patched various holes the disaster had caused to open in the sky, thereby making it stronger than ever.

Emergence of the Culture Heroes

Thanks to Nuwa's quick thinking and creative skills, the humans survived, and as a result, over the many centuries that followed, they gave rise to one generation after another. Nevertheless, there was no guarantee that they would be clever, hardworking, and tenacious enough to construct a civilized society. Fashioning the diverse aspects of human civilization turned out to be the third major element of creation in Chinese mythology. These included the adoption of agriculture, organized religion, the establishment of government and laws, and the invention of various arts, crafts, literature, and so forth.

The ancient Chinese called the creators of these aspects of civilized life culture heroes. Among the earliest of their number recognized in myths were Nuwa, her brother (or in some accounts, her mate) Fuxi, and Shennong, a local ruler who was later worshipped as a god. The ancient Chinese came to group these three legendary characters together, collectively calling them the Three Divine Sovereigns (or Three Sage-Kings).

Nuwa, for instance, not only created the first humans and introduced the crucial social custom of marriage; usually depicted in art with a woman's face and a serpent's body, she also received credit for inventing at least three musical instruments. Among these was the flutelike *shenghuang*, which is still used in traditional Chinese music.

Fuxi, who supposedly had a human's upper body and the lower body of a dragon, was said to be an even more prolific inventor. In one famous tale, he taught humans how to raise domestic animals, hunt, and fish. At first, the story went, a dragon that then ruled the oceans initially objected to letting people catch fish, for fear that the human fishers might remove *all* the fish, leaving the seas barren. Later, the dragon learned that the fish could reproduce faster than humans could catch them, so he no longer viewed human fishers as a threat. Fuxi was also said to have invented the *qin* (pronounced 'chin'), a seven-stringed musical instrument that one plays by plucking the strings.

The third Divine Sovereign, Shennong, whose name means "Spirit Farmer" in Chinese, was traditionally credited with creating the first plow. The first marketplace, where people could buy

qin
A seven-stringed musical instrument that one plays by plucking

By tasting and testing various herbs, Shennong (pictured) was able to discover their medicinal properties.

and sell food, clothes, and other items, was also reported to be his idea. His biggest claim to fame, however, was in the area of medicine, particularly those cures made from herbs. According to Yang and An, Shennong found, tasted, and tested

> hundreds of herbs in order to figure out their medicinal characteristics and functions. Then he completely knew their flavors and properties of coldness, warmness, mildness, or toxicity, and thereafter used them to cure people's diseases. . . . Shennong is described not only as the [inventor] of Chinese traditional medicine, but also as [the first] general practitioner of medicine.[10]

Modern Religious Worship and Myth Making

Of the many cultural aspects of modern China that were partly shaped by mythology, various religious customs are among the more obvious and important. Indeed, many of the gods who populate the ancient tales are still recognized and worshipped today across China. (Although China's Communist government officially promotes atheism, the country's constitution permits a number of religious groups to worship freely, provided they do not cause social or political disorder.) One of the more popular annual religious observances is the Nuwa Palace Festival, held from March 15 to 18 each year in northern China. Thousands of citizens attend the ceremonies, which include feasting, praying, and watching reenactments of some of Nuwa's ancient myths, including her creating the human race and saving it from extinction. The worshippers also hear selected speakers talk about newer myths associated with that goddess. One such tale, coined in the 1940s during World War II, recounts how a brave Chinese leader became the target of Japanese invaders. Supposedly, Nuwa conjured up an impenetrable fog that gave that leader sufficient cover to escape his pursuers.

Abiding by the Will of the Gods

As explained in the Chinese myths, thanks to the efforts of Nuwa, Fuxi, Shennong, and other culture heroes, humans came into being and built a complex civilization. Yet the gods made sure that people did not overstep their bounds and destroy the natural world in the process. In Chinese mythology, humans in general— from rulers and soldiers to farmers, merchants, craftspeople, and others—most often work within the bounds of and with respect for the sanctity of nature. Humanity's "good fortune," scholars O.B. Duane and N. Hutchison point out, "depended on its ability to behave in accordance with the dictates of Heaven. From ancient times onwards, the highest ambition [humans] could aspire to was to determine the natural law of things and to behave in sympathy with it."[11]

CHAPTER TWO

Legendary Stories of Love and Lovers

When the emperor Wanli ruled China in the late 1500s, the country's capital, Beijing, was crowded, busy, and prosperous. Entertainment centers, including bars and dance halls, were widely popular, and a young woman named Du Shiniang was well known among the city's singers and dancers. For a long time she concentrated on her art and career and had no interest in meeting and falling in love with a young man.

That situation changed one day when Du was walking home from work. In the crowded street, she accidentally bumped into a young scholar named Li Jia, who had only recently moved to Beijing. After apologizing to each other for the minor mishap, they exchanged pleasantries, and Li told her that he found her fascinating. In the days and weeks that followed, they continued to meet in public and told each other about their family backgrounds. It did not take long for Du to fall in love with Li, and he claimed he loved her no less. Soon he moved into the small apartment where Du had been living alone for some time, and the two told people they were husband and wife even though there had been no formal marriage ceremony.

Trouble Follows

Trouble arose, however, when Li's parents discovered that he was living with a dancer, a profession they and most other well-to-do people considered low class. They demanded that he leave Du's apartment and return to their family home. When he refused, they disowned him and refused to pay anymore for his schooling or to give him his usual spending money.

Soon Du admitted to Li that she had recently been making less than usual at work and as a result could no longer afford to pay the rent for her apartment. Forced to move out, all the couple could afford to rent was a small boat docked on the city's Houhai Lake. One day, while on the boat, Du sang one of her favorite songs, and a wealthy man named Sun Fu, who lived nearby,

One of China's best-known love stories takes place during the reign of emperor Wanli (pictured). The tale involves a popular dancer who falls in love with a young scholar.

heard her. He walked to the dock, saw how beautiful she was, and decided that she should be with him instead of Li. The next day, after Du had left for work, Sun and Li met and talked. Sun said he would give Li a lot of money if he left Du and never came back. Li agreed to the deal.

What the two men did not realize was that Du had only pretended to go to work and had overheard the conversation. She was stunned that Li did not love her as deeply as she loved him and that he would stoop to taking Sun's money and leaving her. Hurt and furious, Du suddenly revealed that she had also lied. She had been saving most of her salary for years and had a big chest full of money that she had planned to surprise Li with soon. But now that she had learned how unfaithful he was, she would not allow him to enjoy that money. As quoted in a modern retelling of the story for China's English-language newspaper *China Daily*, Du told him, "I hid my wealth in the chest, as I wanted to see if you loved me truly. I meant to use it when we started our family. How you have disappointed me! After a few coaxing words [from Sun], you . . . betrayed me!"[12] At that tense moment, Du pushed the chest into the lake, then jumped in and drowned herself.

A Country of Romantic Folk

For thousands of years, the Chinese have passed the story of Du and Li from one generation to the next. In general, people have tended to admire Du for her strong moral character and to dislike Li for betraying her. Their myth has become a cautionary tale. It warns that a truly loving relationship requires both parties to be fully committed to each other and that the foundation of such a union is mutual trust.

Du and Li's myth is only one of several kinds of love story that developed in China over the centuries. While it deals with misplaced trust and betrayal, others explore relationships in which mutual trust exists but circumstances keep the lovers apart. And still other tales tell how the two parties manage to overcome their problems and live happily ever after.

Whatever their approach and outcome, the sheer number of Chinese myths involving love and lovers is remarkable. According to one expert Chinese observer, "There are literally hundreds of love stories in Chinese culture." The reason is that "China is a nation of romantics. Chinese people adore love stories and have communally passed down many ancient tales of romance and love through the generations."[13]

A Pair of Butterflies

Among those many love myths is the popular tale about Liang Shanbo and Zhu Yingtai, also known as the Butterfly Lovers. In their story Zhu grows up as the clever but spoiled daughter of a

A Long-Lived Tale

In an article about the myth of the Butterfly Lovers, Chinese scholar Minjie Su points out that this tale is a very old one in China. Here, she briefly traces the main mentions of the myth in ancient Chinese writings.

The earliest written record of the lovers is traced back to about 700 AD, when the Empress Wu Zetian (624–705) reigned. . . . The lovers' names only appear in one sentence, saying that they are buried together. The story is entirely glossed over, but this record, although brief, attests to the long history and popularity of the tale. It must have been so well-known at that time that the author deems it unnecessary to recount the story. A slightly expanded version is found in the 9th century. . . . It tells the bulk of the story and anchors Zhu's loyalty and bravery . . . [and she] becomes the dominant character of the [myth]. This perhaps has something to do with her rebellious spirit. After all, no ordinary girl would demand to go to school in an era when literacy and knowledge were denied to girls, forcing her to live among men and pretend to be one of them.

Minjie Su, "The Butterfly Lovers: A Classic Chinese Love Story," 2022. Medievalists.net. www.medievalists.net.

wealthy Chinese government official. In the society of that era, girls are not allowed to go to school, a privilege allotted only to boys from well-to-do families.

Zhu refuses to accept this social custom. She sneaks out of her parents' home, disguises herself as a boy, and manages to enroll in a nearby widely respected school. In the late afternoon each day, she returns home and changes back into her female clothing. All the while, her mother and father have no inkling of what is happening.

At school Zhu meets a young man named Liang Shanbo. They are instantly drawn to each other and quickly become best

In the Butterfly Lovers tale (commemorated in a special set of postage stamps) a young woman dresses as a boy so that she can attend school. While there she meets the love of her life.

化蝶双飞 (5—5) T

friends. In the three years that ensue, the two spend many hours together each week. Despite their closeness, Liang does not realize that Zhu is a girl.

Then one day Zhu's father tells her that he has arranged for her to marry a young man from a neighboring town, an individual she has never even met. Moreover, her parents force her to help them full time with the wedding preparations, leaving no time for her clandestine schooling or visits with Liang.

Liang becomes so worried about his friend's absence that one day after his classes he goes to Zhu's family home and asks to see the owner's son. When told by a servant that the owner has a daughter not a son, Liang finally realizes that Zhu is actually female. That does not change his feelings for her, however, and he meets with Zhu's parents and tells them he wants to marry her. He is crestfallen when they reject him because, they point out, his own parents are not well-to-do enough.

Distraught and grief stricken, Liang refuses to eat or drink anything. Within a few weeks he dies, but not before arranging for his coffin to be placed on the side of the road that Zhu's wedding party is scheduled to pass. Chinese scholar Minjie Su tells what happens next:

> When the appointed day arrives, Zhu is escorted to her fiancé's house to complete the wedding ceremony. A raging storm suddenly breaks out, and the marriage procession has no choice but to stop by Liang's grave. The lady steps out of the litter to mourn her lover, richly dressed in her scarlet bridal dress and adored with dazzling jewels, as if she were really the dead man's bride. Seeing that the tomb opens at her coming, the lady throws herself in without hesitation. The sky soon clears, and the sun shines again, but to the amazement of those present, the bride is no more. Instead, a pair of butterflies are seen fluttering around the grave before they disappear into the distance.[14]

The Cloud Weaver and the Cowherd

That concept—of two lovers belonging with each other for eternity—appears in another myth. It is the heartwarming tale of the lovers Zhi Nu and Niu Lang. Many centuries ago, the story goes, the stars visible in the night sky were the shiny life forces of angel-like beings who did the bidding of the Queen Mother, the powerful goddess who controlled the sky.

One day the Queen Mother noticed that two of her angels—Niu Lang, the spirit of the masculine star Altair, and Zhi Nu, the spirit of the feminine star Vega—had fallen deeply in love. The goddess frowned on such romances because she felt they interfered with her total control of the heavenly vault that stretched over the earth. Deciding to punish the celestial lovers, the Queen Mother first demoted Zhi. The former bright and silvery star Vega became a minor nature spirit called a "cloud weaver." Niu's star was transformed into a lowly human cowherd in an earthly village.

The reactions of the former lovers were predictable. In the words of modern Chinese storyteller Shuang Ying Han, Zhi's "face was always awash with tears and she could find no consolation in her loneliness."[15] As for Niu, he bore a perpetually sad expression, and never an hour went by that he did not daydream about seeing his beloved Zhi once again. Moreover, over time Niu fell into abject poverty. All he had left in the world were a wobbly wooden wagon and an aging, talking cow that became his only companion. The young cowherd and his cow dwelled in a small, broken-down shack far from the nearest town. As Niu's desolation grew, he even stopped talking to his cow.

A Passionate Cry of True Love

One day, however, the cow broke the silence. It told Niu that he should journey several miles to the east to a place called the Lotus Garden. There he would see some female nature spirits

In one famous myth, two separated lovers reunite at a lotus garden, like the one shown here, with the help of a talking cow.

swimming and frolicking in the garden's ponds, and Zhi would be among them. In a moment of weakness, the cow explained, the Queen Mother had generously allowed the unhappy cloud weaver to visit that pleasant place.

Niu asked the cow how it could possibly know such things. The cow answered that his question would be answered in good time, but until then Niu would have to trust the accuracy of the information. Because the cow had never led him astray, Niu accepted its word and journeyed to the Lotus Garden. Sure enough, when he arrived, he saw the nature spirits swimming and relaxing. One of them seemed to recognize him, and when she walked up to him, he realized that she was indeed his beloved Zhi.

After a joyous reunion, the lovers vowed never to be separated again. To help cement their bond, they married and moved into the small house that Niu shared with the cow. To make their livings, Niu raised crops, aided by his faithful bovine friend, and Zhi wove cotton and made clothes.

Several years later, the cow passed away, but shortly before its death it finally revealed to Niu its long-held secret. Like its two human friends, it too had once dwelled in the night sky—as the well-known constellation Taurus the bull. It had chosen to follow Niu to earth to protect him during his years of exile and to that end had taken the form of a cow.

On the same day the cow died, the Queen Mother appeared and said that Zhi's punishment was over and that she could return to the sky. But Niu would have to remain in human form on earth for a long time to come. This decision by the goddess did not stand, however. According to a modern retelling of the tale, right after the Queen Mother escorted Zhi back into the sky, "the couple cried out for each other with all of their passion."[16]

Celebration of the Moon Goddess

One of China's most popular holidays, the Mid-autumn Festival, is based largely on the myth about the moon goddess Chang'e. In the story she is the human wife of a brave archer named Yi. After he shoots down nine of the ten suns that have been steadily destroying the earth, as a reward a god gives him a vial of liquid that confers immortality on anyone who drinks it. Because Yi and his wife love each other so much, he does not want to drink the elixir. After all, if he does, he will have to watch her grow old and die while he remains young and vital. Later, not knowing what is in the vial, Chang'e swallows the liquid, which causes her to float up into the sky. Worried that she will drift farther and farther away and never see Yi again, she transforms into the moon, so she will always be near the earth and her beloved.

The yearly Chinese holiday honoring Chang'e features a friendly atmosphere in which the celebrants share meals and drinks and leave out fruits, desserts, and other tasty items on open-air altars. The common belief is that Chang'e appreciates these treats and blesses those who offer them.

At that moment the goddess finally grasped the depth of their feelings toward each other. The Queen Mother was so moved by this display of love that she allowed Niu to return to the heavens with his beloved Zhi.

This heartwarming story has survived the march of the centuries. On the anniversary of the day the lovers were reunited, young women in China make wishes on the stars Vega and Altair, hoping to have loved-filled futures with their boyfriend or husband. That special activity lies at the core of China's version of Valentine's Day. Called the Qixi (pronounced "chi-shee") Festival, it is celebrated on the seventh day of the seventh month of the Chinese lunar calendar.

Chang'e

The Chinese goddess of the moon, who floated into the sky after drinking a magic elixir

CHAPTER THREE

Tales of Warriors, Weapons, and War

In the vast corpus, or collection, of Chinese myths, four strong beings were said to have guarded ancient China's outer borders. One was a huge dragon that protected the eastern border; the second was a giant white tiger standing guard in the west; the third was a tall, bright red bird that dwelled in the south; and lastly, the fourth protector was Xuan Wu, more often called the Black Warrior, thought to be the defender of the north.

In his principal myth, Xuan Wu started out as a prince in the royal family of a very ancient kingdom. As a young man, he wanted to become a scholar, and he set out to find a proper school for his education. He heard that such a school existed in a religious temple situated atop a high peak known as Wu-dang Mountain.

Xuan Wu exerted great effort as he climbed up the steep slope leading to the school. Once there he studied for several years, and in the course of time he became highly versed in weaponry and the art of war. That earned him a widespread reputation as the so-called Perfect Warrior.

At one point the leader of the Chinese gods—the Jade Emperor—decided it was time to test Xuan Wu. The man's fighting skills were not in question; in fact, no other human's could surpass them. Rather, the test was designed to determine whether, under certain circumstances, the great warrior could preserve human life as avidly as he could take it.

One day when Xuan Wu was quietly meditating near the edge of a tall cliff, the chief god sent a woman to him. She offered to brush the Perfect Warrior's hair, and because he was concentrating so deeply, she startled him. He abruptly flinched, in the process pushing her off the cliff. Suddenly realizing what had happened, without hesitation Xuan Wu dove over the edge in an attempt to save her. In this way he passed the test. Fortunately, no one died that day, because the gods sent flying dragons to rescue the falling woman and to whisk Xuan Wu up to heaven. Thereafter, he was the divine Black Warrior who protected China's northern flank.

Creation of the War God

Warriors like Xuan Wu, the weapons they wielded, and the wars they fought were ever-present realities not only in ancient China but in Chinese mythology as well. The importance of battles, soldiers, and warfare in the myths was reflected not only in the tale of the Perfect Warrior but also in dozens of other stories. One of the more familiar ones—to the Chinese of the present as well as the past—dates from a dimly remembered ancient era. It tells how a Chinese national government selected a well-respected historical military general—Guan Yu—and proceeded to deify him; that is, make him divine. Moreover, he became not just some minor or inconsequential deity but rather the widely respected and feared god of war. "At the grassroots level of society," Chinese scholar Wu Haiyun writes,

Guan Yu
The ancient Chinese god of war

Guan Yu became a kind of patron saint or protector god for everyone from blacksmiths and opera performers to . . . police officers. [In addition] so many merchants started worshipping Guan Yu, he's become one of China's four main wealth gods. What explains Guan Yu's almost supernatural popularity, capable of bringing together cops and criminals, emperors and commoners?[17]

The highly respected general Guan Yu (pictured) gained divine status, becoming the feared god of war. He was also adopted as a protector god.

The answer to that question, Haiyun explains, was Guan Yu's powerful sense of loyalty to the country's leaders and their system of dictatorial rule. His "bullheaded adherence to the principle of [loyalty to the state] proved key to his meteoric rise." she continues. "China's emperors, who valued loyalty in their subjects, saw Guan Yu's obedience and respect for his superiors as a value worth propagating."[18]

The fact that the Chinese initially had no national war god and eventually felt compelled to create one says much about the importance of war in ancient China. Indeed, says historian Mark Cartwright, the ancient Chinese kingdoms and city-states saw a great deal of military competition between city-rulers eager to grab the riches of their neighbors, and there is no doubt that success in this endeavor legitimized reigns and increased the welfare of the victors and their people. Those who did not fight had their possessions taken, their dwellings destroyed and were usually either enslaved or killed. Indeed, much of China's history thereafter involves wars between one state or another.[19]

One of the Biggest Mythical Wars

The themes of warriors, weapons, and war were therefore bound to be mirrored in the myths the ancient Chinese passed along from one generation to another. Of those traditional tales, perhaps

Weapons Mentioned in the Myths

Various weapons are described frequently in the ancient Chinese myths about warriors and wars. As might be expected, the weapons mentioned in these tales are the ones that were then current in real Chinese warfare. By far the most common was the bow, made especially famous in the myth of the warrior Yi, the skilled archer who shot nine of the original suns from the sky with his trusty bow and arrows. The Chinese employed crude bows back in the Stone Age and began using a more advanced version—the composite bow—in about 1600 BCE. An even more lethal version sometimes mentioned in myths—the crossbow—appeared in China sometime between 450 and 300 BCE.

In some mythical battles, warriors fought with swords. According to historian Mark Cartwright, swords "appeared relatively late on Chinese battlefields, probably from around 500 BCE, and never quite challenged the bow or crossbow as the prestige weapons of Chinese armies. Developing from long-bladed daggers and spearheads which were used for stabbing, the true sword was made from bronze and then, later, iron."

Mark Cartwright, "Ancient Chinese Warfare," *World History Encyclopedia*, November 7, 2017. www.worldhistory.org.

none was more popular and enduring than those surrounding the exploits of the legendary Huang-di, also known as the Yellow Emperor. All sorts of colorful stories were told about him. For instance, supposedly he ruled for a hundred years or more. Also, he was credited with giving rise to dozens of later emperors and was remembered as one of China's greatest culture heroes, who was said to have invented the calendar, ships, music, and much more. Finally, his myths claim, in his old age he turned into a gigantic dragon and flew up into the heavens.

As exciting and romantic as these stories were and remain, Huang-di is most remembered for his role in one of ancient China's biggest and most decisive mythical wars. At the time, the story goes, he ruled a sprawling kingdom in central China. A few years before that, he and another war leader, known as the Red Emperor, had vied for power, and the Yellow Emperor had soundly defeated

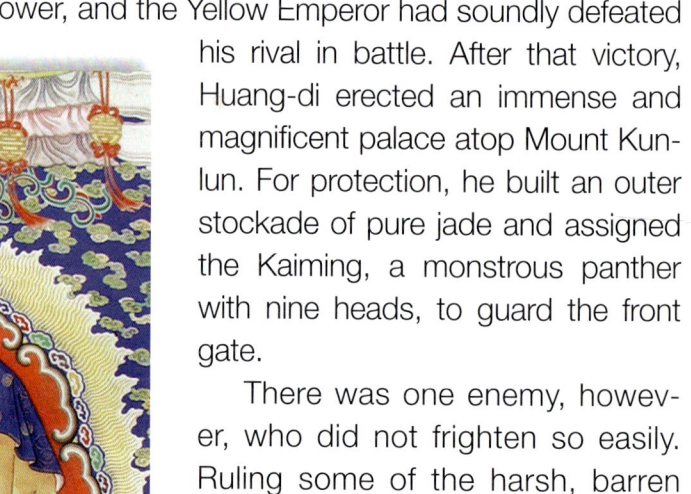

his rival in battle. After that victory, Huang-di erected an immense and magnificent palace atop Mount Kunlun. For protection, he built an outer stockade of pure jade and assigned the Kaiming, a monstrous panther with nine heads, to guard the front gate.

There was one enemy, however, who did not frighten so easily. Ruling some of the harsh, barren lands lying beyond China's borders was a godlike but repulsive being named Chi-you. He was the eldest of seventy-two brothers, all

The legendary Yellow Emperor (pictured) defeated a god-like yet repulsive being by assembling a huge army of human, animal, and ghost fighters.

of whom were misshapen and frightening in various ways. According to O.B. Duane and N. Hutchison:

> They each spoke the language of humans, but their bodies below the neckline were those of animals with cloven [split] feet. Their heads were made of iron and their hideous copper faces contained four repulsive eyeballs protruding from mottled foreheads. These brothers . . . liked to eat stones and chunks of metal, and their special skill was the manufacture of battle weapons, including sharp lances, spears, axes, shields, and strong bows.[20]

Days of Appalling Violence

Chi-you was eager to conquer and enslave the Chinese people, and to that end he assembled a huge army. Hearing of the approach of that horde, Huang-di gathered an army of his own. Each of the opposing forces included human fighters and various nature gods, ghosts, bears, and tigers.

In a large meadow located in central China, the two vast armies clashed with appalling violence. For several days they fought without producing a clear-cut victor, and both leaders grew increasingly frustrated. Finally, Chi-you decided it was time to fight in a dishonorable manner. Using a diabolical magic spell, he created a mass of thick fog that rapidly spread across the battlefield and enveloped large portions of the Yellow Emperor's soldiers. "The dense blanket of cloud," Duane and Hutchison write, "swirled around them, completely obscuring their vision, and they began to stab blindly with their weapons at the thin air. Then suddenly, the wild animals who made up a large part of the emperor's forces started to panic and to flee in every direction."[21]

Upset by this turn of events, Huang-di sought a way to remove the fog and even the odds but to no avail. He then hurried to his military advisers, which included a minor god named Feng-hou. Well known at the time for his cleverness and knowledge of warfare, Feng-hou studied the situation intently and within mere minutes suggested a solution. What was needed, he said, was a device that would always point in the same direction, no matter the position in which one held it. Today people call it a compass. But at the time it was called the "south-pointing chariot." With such an instrument, Feng-hou explained, Huang-di's forces could stop wandering aimlessly through the fog and find their way out of it.

Huang-di immediately approved the plan, and Feng-hou employed his divine powers to fashion the south-pointing chariot. Sure enough, only a few hours after the Yellow Emperor's fighters began using the device, they made it out of the thick fog and into the daylight. There the battle once more raged, and within a few hours it appeared that Huang-di's forces might be winning.

Now angrier and more frustrated than ever, Chi-you used every ounce of his magical abilities to fight back. This time he conjured up a massive thunderstorm that dumped enormous amounts of rain on Huang-di's fighters. At first they started to fall back, but then Huang-di retaliated with a unique weapon of his own. It took the form of the gigantic dragon-shaped deity Ying Long. That fearsome being charged forward, and in Duane and Hutchison's words, "hundreds of enemy bodies were crushed beneath his giant feet." Eventually, "the casualties were too heavy for Chi-you to bear [and] he called for his remaining [soldiers] to withdraw from the fighting."[22]

Detailed Replicas of Huang-di's Warriors

Many of the exploits credited to Huang-di involve magic and divine intervention. Although these stories are clearly mythical, historians have shown that he was a real historical figure and may have been one of China's earliest rulers. The myths describing his wars, including the one with the villainous Chi-you, make frequent mention of the soldiers who fought in the opposing armies. A revealing perspective on such early Chinese warriors came to light in March 1974. Chinese archaeologists uncovered a massive collection of life-size, terra-cotta soldiers at Xian, in east-central China. Including the full-size replicas of those warriors' horses, there are thousands of sculpted figures arrayed in a tomb that appears to be that of the real Huang-di. The figures weigh up to 600 pounds (272 kg) each. Furthermore, they are not all cookie-cutter images made from a single mold. Rather, each is unique and highly detailed, thereby revealing to modern observers the clothing, armor, and even hairstyles of soldiers in that remote era.

Immortality in a Distant Future

No one knows whether the legendary war between Huang-di and Chi-you was based on memories of a real war in China's distant past. In contrast, at least one well-documented war generated several related myths. Among them is the widely popular story of the female hero Hua Mulan, often called Mulan for short. The conflict occurred sometime between 386 and 534 CE, during a period in which China was ruled by the Wei dynasty. Opposing the Wei armies in the war was an early Mongolian people known as the Rouran.

When the Rouran invaded China from the north, the Wei ruler issued a decree that ordered every Chinese family to contribute at least one male fighter for the army. For some families, among them Mulan's family, fulfilling this order posed great difficulty. Mulan's father was old and infirm, and his son was a small child. So neither of them could fight. To compensate, Mulan, then in her late teens and full of vigor, told her father that she would fight in his stead. To that end, she dressed in men's armor and swiftly gathered the necessary equipment. A written work of that period, *The Ballad of Mulan*, has survived and says in part, "In the East Market she buys a spirited horse; in the West Market she buys a saddle; in the South Market she buys a bridle; in the North Market she buys a long whip. At dawn she takes leave of Father."[23]

The legendary warrior Mulan began her heroic journey after deciding to take the place of her frail father on the battlefield. Dressed in men's armor, she fooled the military into believing she was a male soldier.

With the armor and weapons she had gathered, Mulan was able to fool the military recruiters into thinking she was a male soldier, and they accepted her into the army's ranks. Subsequently, the ballad states, the brave young woman went "ten thousand miles on the business of war [and crossed over] mountains like flying northern [wind] gusts." Over the course of ten years she witnessed officers and ordinary soldiers alike "die in a hundred battles."[24]

When she finally returned to the Chinese capital, Mulan personally met with the Wei emperor. He was so impressed with her courageous exploits (although he still had no idea his gallant solider was a woman) that he offered her a position in his government as a reward. She politely refused, telling him, "[I have] no use for a minister's post. I wish to ride a swift mount to take me back to my home."[25] Reunited with her family, Mulan removed her male attire and once more dressed as a woman.

As time went by, her secret got out, and in the generations that followed, she became a legend in China. Later still, in the fullness of time, that ancient land, along with others around the globe, gave way to technologically advanced societies. And in that distant future, Mulan and her accomplishments remained widely known and popular, giving her a sort of immortality that neither she nor anyone she knew in her own day could have foreseen or even imagined.

CHAPTER FOUR

A Proud Legacy of Mythical Heroes

Long, long ago, at the very dawn of time, a mighty deity named Dijun ruled the sky. He had ten children, each of whom was a very bright, very hot sun. By order of their divine father, they took turns, so that each day only one of them crossed the sky. A day finally came, however, when the children decided to break the rule their father had set. They all entered the sky at the same time, and the result was widespread misery and death as the earth's surface was relentlessly scorched. As O.B. Duane and N. Hutchison tell it:

> Crops began to wilt, rivers began to dry up, food became scarce, and people began to suffer burns and wretched hunger pangs. They prayed for rains to drive away the suns, but none appeared. . . . They hid beneath the great trees of the forests for shade, but these were stripped of leaves and offered little or no protection. And now great hungry beasts of prey and dreaded monsters emerged from the wilderness and began to devour the human beings they encountered.[26]

When all seemed lost, however, a brave man named Yi, who was an expert archer, became determined to end the disaster. He gathered his powerful bow and trusty arrows and strode out onto an open plain, above which all ten glowing orbs could be seen floating. For several minutes, Yi glared at the shining balls of light, making calculations in his mind about how best to aim his arrows for maximum impact against them. Then, according to scholar Cyril Birch, the fearless

hero "placed an arrow against the bowstring and drew to the full . . . [with] the muscles leaping on his arms. Squinting upwards, he loosed the shaft."[27] The missile shot upward, higher and higher until it pierced one of the suns, which suddenly exploded in a dazzling display, went dark, and fell headlong into the sea. After that, one by one, Yi shot down eight more of the searing suns, leaving the single one known today, and thereby he rescued the world and humanity.

In saving the world and humankind from fiery destruction, Yi has ever since been hailed as a hero of the first magnitude in the annals of Chinese mythology. That massive corpus of tales is also replete with other sorts of heroes. Anne Birrell notes that there are culture heroes such as Nuwa, Fuxi, and Shennong, who introduced new aspects of civilized life. She explains that there are also heroes distinguished by "acts of military courage, idealism, devotion to a cause, [and] nobility of spirit,"[28] as well as heroes who are great patriots, monster killers, successful warriors on the battlefield, and saviors of individuals, communities, and even civilization as a whole. The culture hero Nuwa is also known as a great savior for her heroic act of rescuing humanity from the collapsing sky.

A Strange Premonition

Not every such savior acted on such a grand scale. One of the more memorable heroes from Chinese mythology is the kindly Buddhist monk Ji Gong. Born to a rich family, he rejected the benefits of inherited wealth. Instead, he embraced poverty, dedicating himself to helping the poor, infirm, and others in need. His tale has been immortalized in modern times in ballets, plays, and other reenactments titled *Ji Gong Abducts the Bride*.

In the story's opening, one day Ji was on his way from his monastery to a local village when he suddenly had a strange premonition. Somehow he sensed that something terrible was going to happen soon. Concentrating as hard as he could, he managed to visualize a few seconds of the immediate future and saw that an earth tremor would cause a nearby mountain peak to break off. The monstrous avalanche it would create would then roll downhill and utterly destroy the village below, killing all its inhabitants.

Having witnessed that frightening event to come, Ji hurried into the village and ran from street to street, shouting for the residents to flee. Within minutes they would suffer horrible deaths, he said. But these warnings fell on deaf ears. It was a perfectly calm, quiet, sunny day, one villager told him, speaking for his neighbors as well as himself. How could something terrible occur on such a peaceful day in the countryside? the man asked the distraught monk.

For a moment Ji worried that nothing could be done in time to save the village and that the situation was therefore hopeless. In the next instant, however, he noticed a group of wedding guests marching

One memorable tale from Chinese mythology revolves around the Buddhist monk Ji Gong (pictured). Born into wealth, he embraced poverty and dedicated his life to assisting those less fortunate and in need.

A Loyal and Victorious General

One of China's most beloved mythical heroes, Yue Fei, was said to have lived in the 1100s CE, when faraway Europe was in the midst of its medieval period. During that century, a warlike people from the region north of China attacked several Chinese cities, and Yue Fei was one of the military generals who defended those cities. A surviving poem about him penned in that period claims that he angrily reacted to the invasion, saying, "The national insult is yet to be avenged!" He added, "Let us ride the long chariots to crush [the enemy's] mountain strongholds, [and] let us start to take back our rivers and mountains." Before his first battle with the invaders, supposedly Yue's mother tattooed the following words on his upper back: "Serve the country loyally." He then went on to crush the enemy in battle after battle. One of the many tales about him says that with an army of only five hundred soldiers, he slew tens of thousands of the intruders, thereby forever cementing his mythical legacy.

Quoted in Deng Yinke, *History of China*, trans. Martha Avery and Pan Yue. Beijing: China Intercontinental, 2007, p. 113.

along the street, evidently on their way to perform the marriage ceremony. Thinking quickly, the desperate monk ran over to the colorfully dressed bride, grabbed hold of her, tossed her over his shoulder, and ran away with her.

Startled and upset, the groom gave chase, as did the other marchers, who as they ran called out to their neighbors to help retrieve the stolen bride. Less than a minute later, everyone in the village had exited the village gate in hot pursuit of what they thought was a holy man turned kidnapper. It was then that a horrendous rumbling noise echoed across the landscape, and some villagers turned to see the entire top of the nearby mountain collapse. Giant boulders rushed down the slopes and smashed into the village, flattening every structure and sending pieces of debris flying in all directions. Clearly, by making the residents chase him into the countryside, Ji had saved all their lives. And in the days that followed, each of them thanked him heartily.

Rise of a Moral Hero

Ji's heroics were clearly centered on overt physical actions, especially his attempts to convince the villagers to flee and his audacious seizure of the bride. Another and far less physical kind of heroic figure seen in a number of Chinese myths tended to set ethical examples for others. That kind of character is therefore frequently referred to as a "moral hero."

Among the more renowned moral heroes in China's ancient annals was a man named Shun (sometimes called Hibiscus), who rose from humble beginnings to the corridors of political power thanks to his highly unusual character. From an early age he displayed an innate sense of decency and friendliness and in Tao Tao Liu Sanders's words "had an extraordinary effect on all the other people he met. Wherever he went he was welcomed . . . and under his influence [people] forgot their quarrels and started to work together."[29]

Shun

A likely fictional early Chinese hero and emperor who legends claimed ruled sometime between 2258 and 2195 BCE

The only exceptions to this rule were Shun's father, mother, and brother. When he was a boy they treated him cruelly, mostly because they were insanely jealous of him. They also attempted to kill him several times. They tried to drown him in a well, burn him in a barn, and get him so drunk that he could easily be stabbed to death. All of these attempts failed, however.

These happenings came to the attention of the reigning emperor, Yao, who sent word that he wanted to meet Shun. At their first meeting, Yao was instantly impressed. The two became fast friends, and less than a year later the emperor went so far as to name Shun as his successor to the throne. In the fullness of time, Shun did indeed become China's ruler, and his moral goodness set a powerful example for his subjects. In their eyes the act that made him appear most heroic of all was the manner in which he dealt with his family. Instead of punishing his spite-

Shun rose from humble beginnings to become one of China's emperors. His moral goodness set a powerful example for his subjects.

ful relatives, as most rulers surely would have done, he publicly forgave them, and as a result they regretted their actions and became better people.

Lady Mu Takes Charge

China suffered no incursions of enemy armies during Shun's reign, so he never had to prove his heroic qualities on the battlefield. Nevertheless, Chinese mythology does have its share of military heroes, and one of the greatest of their number was a woman. Named Lady Mu Guiying, she made her mark in the 1100s CE, when a line of rulers belonging to the Song dynasty held power.

The exploits of Lady Mu Guiying are immortalized in a popular Chinese opera. As a general in China's military, she showed her soldiers a way to destroy the enemy and save China.

Although China was populous and prosperous during the Song dynasty, the country was sometimes plagued by invaders from the north. The Chinese viewed these invaders as barbarians who intended to destroy civil society. The invaders, whom the Chinese called Xiongnu, had developed a new and dangerous military formation. The manner in which it worked has not survived, although its name has: people called this formation the Heavenly Gate Array.

The commander of China's army, General Yang Yanzhao, tried several times to break the Heavenly Gate Array but failed and lost hundreds of soldiers in each attempt. It looked like the victorious Xiongnu might next march on the Chinese heartland and slaughter many thousands of farmers, merchants, and others. In desperation, Yang called forth his grown son, Yang Zongbao, and ordered him to seek out Mu Guiying, who dwelled in a village in some nearby mountains. Mu came from a military family, and it was said that over the years she had accumulated a great deal of knowledge about war and battlefield tactics. Furthermore, she had sent messages to various Chinese

Xiongnu

A warlike people who occupied parts of Mongolia from the third century BCE to the first century CE

Mu Conquers Modern Popular Culture

"In modern Chinese pop entertainment," writes East Asian online movie critic Ced Yong, "Mu Guiying is hands-down the most frequently depicted folkloric heroine. Since the 1980s, there have been over ten depictions of her in East Asian pop entertainment." Indeed, Mu Guiying, who is credited in mythology with breaking the deadly battlefield formation of the invading Xiongnu, is one of the most often depicted mythological characters in modern popular culture. Among the entertainment media to which Yong refers are TV miniseries, one of which aired in 1994. Titled *Heroic Legend of the Yang's Family*, the lavish Chinese production chronicled the complex interactions among the male and female heroes, including Mu, who resisted the invaders. Four years later a Hong Kong production, *The Heroine of the Yangs*, focused primarily on Mu's adventures. Noted Chinese actress Amy Chan played Mu. Later, in 2012 a thirty-nine-episode TV series, *Mu Guiying Takes Command*, gained a large viewing audience. It was based directly on multiple operas and ballets with the same title produced as far back as 1959, as well as several graphic novels dealing with Mu's story.

Ced Yong, "5 Legendary Chinese Female Warriors and Heroines. How Many Existed in History?," Owlcation, February 6, 2022. https://owlcation.com.

officers, saying that she knew how to break the Xiongnu's Heavenly Gate Array. Neither Yang Yanzhao nor his son was certain that Mu actually possessed the secret to breaking that formation. But they reasoned that it was worth a try if it might save China from being overrun by the barbarians.

To that end, Yang Zongbao traveled to Mu's village and spoke with her. In an unexpected twist of fate, she fell in love with him at first sight. Moreover, she said she would reveal how to break the enemy's formation only if Yang Zongbao married her. He agreed to do so, and the wedding ceremony followed in less than an hour.

The next day the young couple journeyed to Yang Yanzhao's camp, and Yang Zongbao introduced his new wife to his father. The son said he had every confidence in Mu's abilities as a general and advised the father to turn the army over to her. Feeling he had nothing to lose, Yang Yanzhao did just that; he gave Mu complete charge of the Chinese army.

Yang Yanzhao never regretted that move. After taking command, Mu taught the soldiers the tactics required to destroy the enemy formation and actually led them in the climactic battle. Mu and her fighters handily defeated the Xiongnu, who fled into what is now Mongolia. "Having gained complete victory," *Shanghai Daily* journalist and storyteller Song Xinyi writes, "Mu is recognized as one of the greatest generals in China's history."[30] And by default, that places her on the same pedestal on which the country's finest male heroes stand.

CHAPTER FIVE

China's Mythical Animals and Monsters

A number of ancient Chinese myths describe a massive flood that swept over the earth's surface in the dim past. As Cyril Birch tells it:

> The rivers broke their banks. The dwellers in the plains and valleys, and all who lived by lake or sea shore, saw the waters surge towards them or slowly rise at their feet. [Some people] made rough nests for themselves in the topmost branches of trees—anything anywhere to reach a height, to be out of reach of the swirling, menacing waters. . . . Every man became a fisherman, for meat was no longer to be had.[31]

The catastrophe's survivors also lacked rice and grains because the floodwaters had drowned all the crops people normally planted and harvested. There seemed to be no way to find the seeds that would be needed to create new harvests. It was only because of the bravery of a single animal—a dog—that humans were able to grow and eat crops such as rice again.

That enterprising pup began life as a hunting dog whose task, after the flood, was to go into the marshes with his master and other human hunters and retrieve the birds and other

small animals the men shot with their bows and arrows. One day the dog saw that its master had managed to bring down a large, plump duck. And the four-legged helper eagerly ran through the shallow water until it found the feathered carcass.

Chinese mythology features several different versions of what the dog did next. In one of the more popular ones, while trying to get a strong grip on the duck, the pup stepped farther out into the marsh than usual. The water was deeper there, and for a moment he sank downward into the thick mud lying beneath. Startled but unafraid, he swam back up to the surface, still clutching the feathered prize.

What the dog did not realize was that in the seconds in which he had struggled in the deep mud, something had stuck to his tail. It was a cluster of seeds from rice plants and other crops that the mud had protected during the flood. When the dog brought the duck to his master, the man saw the seeds and rejoiced. He realized that, thanks to his trusty companion, humans would once more be able to grow rice.

Seeds from the Heavens

In some parts of China, the local residents keep alive an alternate version of this myth. In it the hunting dog, along with all other canines, originally possessed nine tails instead of one. Moreover, one day he heard his master complaining about the loss of seeds to grow rice and other crops. Intent on helping his master and other humans, the dog boldly made his way up to the heavens. He reasoned that the gods probably had such seeds, and perhaps he could steal some for the betterment of humanity.

Having made it to the heavens, the pup saw some guards watching a divine farmer plant rice in some pre-dug furrows. The little dog stealthily crept close enough to the furrows that several seeds stuck to each of his nine tails. As he ran away, one of the guards saw him and shot a flaming arrow that burned off eight of the dog's tails. However, the courageous dog kept on running and made it back to the earth's surface with one tail, along with its seeds, intact.

This story supposedly explained two things. One was how dogs ended up with only one tail. The other was how rice agriculture revived on earth and led to a custom during the annual harvest festival when farmers fed their dogs first as way of saying thanks.

A Zoo of Vivid Creatures

Chinese mythology features several other popular myths about dogs. In fact, dogs were only one of many animals that played important roles in China's early folklore. There were also foxes, turtles, birds, and snakes, as well as giants, dragons, and various scary monsters. In the words of Ken Liu, a well-known translator of Chinese tales into English, the corpus of Chinese myths "has a rich menagerie of evocative creatures whose meanings have evolved over time and who are still being invoked and reinterpreted by Chinese writers, game designers, and filmmakers as part of the cultural conversation."[32]

Of all these diverse creatures, foxes are perhaps the most common. The exact reason why foxes were so popular in the myths is lost in the mists of time. Some experts have suggested that it might be that foxes tend to be stealthy and rarely show themselves and thereby can seem mysterious. That might explain why many of the mythical foxes are said to have magical powers or to be tricksters who frequently fooled or tormented people. Several of those mischievous characters are manifestations or versions of China's fox goddess Huxian. People knew she was fox-like due to her name, since in Chinese the root word *hu* means "fox," and the word *xian* translates as "immortal." She was therefore the "immortal fox."

As several other mythical foxes did, Huxian sometimes fooled humans by taking the physical form of a beautiful young woman. In one of her best-known tales, for example, she met a good-looking young man and pretended to be an attractive maiden named Hong-yu. They spent a few nights together, and he fell madly in love with her. Because she was in reality a goddess, she had no interest in a long-term relationship with a human, so after a while she told him he should find someone else.

Still, Huxian was not totally cruel and did pity the young man. So she searched for and found a young woman who agreed to marry him. The story did not have a happy ending, however. Not long after the wedding, a criminal snatched the new wife and, thinking she was doomed anyway, she committed suicide. Moreover, in another horrible twist, the local police, who knew nothing about the kidnapper, accused the husband of killing his young wife. Huxian, still disguised as Hong-yu, managed to persuade the police that the young man was innocent. But he spent the rest of his life unmarried and alone. In the eyes of the ancient Chinese, the moral of the story was that Huxian and other foxes were often troublemakers and not to be trusted.

The Miraculous Panhu

The story of the miraculous dog Panhu is one of the most beloved and popular tales in Chinese mythology. It begins in the dim past in an unnamed Chinese kingdom, the queen of which had recently fallen seriously ill. Her physicians examined her repeatedly but could not determine what was ailing her. At one point it seemed like she might die. But then one day a worm the color of precious gold suddenly crawled out of one of her ears, and after that she quickly recovered. Next the worm underwent several changes of shape until it became a cute, frisky dog. The queen fell instantly in love with the creature, whom she named Panhu. Not long afterward the kingdom went to war against a powerful rival. Panhu proved an invaluable asset to his own land by sneaking into the enemy nation and killing its ruler. On the day the conflict ended, Panhu surprised everyone by speaking in a human voice. He said he desired to marry the royal princess, and when the king and queen hesitated, he further transformed, this time into a handsome human male with a dog's head. The princess then fell in love with Panhu, and their marriage took place.

Quoted in Deng Yinke, *History of China*, trans. Martha Avery and Pan Yue. Beijing: China Intercontinental, 2007, p. 113.

The Four Valiant Dragons

Much more trustworthy than foxes in Chinese myths were dragons. The Greeks, Norse, Hindus, and numerous other ancient peoples mentioned dragons in their myths, but they were typically reptilian monsters that needed slaying. In contrast, most Chinese dragons were benevolent beings who worked to better humanity's lot. The chief model for the Chinese dragon—the *long*—was a very big, powerful, and intelligent creature that in one way or another brought prosperity to human families, communities, and even entire kingdoms.

> **long**
> In Chinese mythology, a large, powerful, benevolent dragon

The tale of the Four Valiant Dragons is a famous example. Sometimes also called the Four Flying Heroes, the story revolves around the Pearl Dragon, Yellow Dragon, Long Dragon, and Black Dragon. The story's backdrop is a lengthy drought that caused crop destruction, famine, and misery in large sections of China. As the dry spell grew increasingly worse, the four dragons felt compassion for the suffering humans and determined to help in whatever way they could.

To that end, the four majestic creatures paid a visit to the chief god—the Jade Emperor—and asked why he had allowed the drought to go on for so long. He replied that he had been very busy lately and that he was actually planning to bring ample rains to the earth soon. Unfortunately for humanity, however, a couple of hours later the Jade Emperor got busy again, and his promise to end the drought slipped his mind.

Some cultures portray dragons as terrible monsters. In Chinese mythology, dragons are viewed as powerful, intelligent, and trustworthy creatures.

A Celebration to Appease the Spirits

Based on the popular ancient myth in which Yang-wang, god of the underworld, gave all ghosts a free pass to visit the earth, China's Ghost Month celebration lasts for about two weeks. It starts on the fifteenth day of the seventh lunar month, so the opening date can vary a little from year to year. The Halloween-like holiday features numerous customs and activities intended in one way or another to appease those disconcerted spirits. In many areas of China, for example, people set up tables in the streets and cover them with a wide range of fruits and meats, hoping the ghosts will appreciate the gesture. Another frequent custom is to burn incense both inside and outside one's house. What is more, because it is thought that ghosts are attracted to water, celebrants employ colored paper to make lanterns in the shape of lotus flowers. They throw these offerings into rivers, where they float downstream, supposedly drawing the spirits back to the underworld.

At that point, the four dragons decided to take care of the problem themselves. They grabbed some giant buckets, soared out over the ocean, and scooped up enormous quantities of water. Then they flew back over the earth's surface and poured the precious liquid onto farmers' parched fields and into dried-up ponds. In addition, the four used some of their potent magical abilities to bring up millions of gallons of water from underground reservoirs. All that extra water went into their subsequent creation of China's largest waterways—the Pearl, Yellow, Black, and Yangtze Rivers.

A Number of Scary Monsters

The fact that the ancient Chinese did not view dragons as scary or malicious monsters did not mean that their myths contained no such monstrous creatures. Indeed, there is no shortage of creepy and frightening beasts in those collected tales. Among them is the Taotie, one of the so-called four evil creatures of the world. (The other three are the flesh-eating Qiongqi; the Taowu, which has big tusks and tries to disrupt human society; and the faceless, yellow-winged Hundun, not to be confused with the primeval creator entity Hundun.)

About the Taotie in particular, writes Liu, the creature is described in various tales as "an extremely greedy beast with an outsized head. It is so ravenous that it ultimately swallowed the rest of its own body, leaving behind only a head. The very name of taotie has become a synonym in Chinese for a glutton."[33] The most commonly repeated myth about the Taotie is its appearance in the story of the war fought between the Chinese general Huang-di and the monster, Chi-you. Supposedly, after Chi-you was defeated and captured. the Chinese beheaded him. And when the head made contact with the ground, it transformed into a Taotie, which quickly ran away to find something to eat.

A number of other scary monsters in Chinese myths were said to inhabit areas that were remote and inaccessible to humans. One of many examples was the Kui, which dwelled in the ocean's depths. It supposedly looked like an ox that had no horns and only one leg. It was so shiny, some stories claimed, that people who looked at it were temporarily blinded. It was also said that the Kui was so heavy that when it dove into the sea, a massive storm was created.

Ghosts in the Attic?

Mentioned far more often in Chinese mythology than the Taotie or the Kui was perhaps the most common and widely feared monster of all—the ghost. Like the ancient Chinese, no small number of modern Chinese still accept that the spirits of dead people

Shown here is an ancient ritual mask of a Taotie, one of the presumed four evil creatures of the world.

routinely roam the landscape. "The ancient Chinese took ghosts very seriously,"[34] writes Chinese educator Sara Lynn Hua. Many Chinese view angry ghosts, she explains, as no less frightening than standard Western mythical monsters like vampires, werewolves, and zombies.

Particularly terrifying in China, Hua points out, is the Nu Gui, which most often translates as "ghost woman." According to various myths, Hua says, she "was wronged in life and is back from the dead to get vengeance by sucking the life essence out of her enemies. These were often the ghosts of women that were murdered or abused by their husbands. Because of that, many urban legends say that these ghosts will kill men but only scare women."[35]

Probably the most famous Chinese myth about ghosts is the one in which Yang-wang, god of the underworld, made a fateful decision. Once each year, he decreed, the souls of deceased people could leave his dark realm and walk the earth. On that day, the ghosts visited their still-living relatives and friends often to haunt and terrify them.

Today all over China people still keep that story alive through the annual celebration of Ghost Month. On that Halloween-like day, mythology briefly becomes a disturbing aspect of real life, as ghosts and other monsters make themselves known to the living, including children in each new generation. Whether it is an irritated spirit thumping in the attic or the Kui hopping on his single foot, Hua says, the traditional sounds of legendary monsters "can often send Chinese children cowering."[36]

SOURCE NOTES

Introduction: A History Highlighted by Greatness

1. O.B. Duane and N. Hutchison, *Chinese Myths and Legends*. London: Brockhampton, 1998, pp. 64, 66.
2. Tao Tao Liu Sanders, *Dragons, Gods, and Spirits from Chinese Mythology*. New York: Peter Bedrick, 1994, p. 11.
3. Sanders, *Dragons, Gods, and Spirits from Chinese Mythology*, p. 12.
4. Anne Birrell, *Chinese Myths*. Austin: University of Texas Press, 2000, p. 15.
5. Birrell, *Chinese Myths*, p. 76.

Chapter One: Pangu, Nuwa, and the World's Creation

6. Cyril Birch, *Tales from China*. New York: Oxford University Press, 2000, p. 2.
7. Lihui Yang and Deming An, *Handbook of Chinese Mythology*. New York: Oxford University Press, 2005, p. 66.
8. Yang and An, *Handbook of Chinese Mythology*, p. 68.
9. Birch, *Tales from China*, p. 3.
10. Yang and An, *Handbook of Chinese Mythology*, p. 71.
11. Duane and Hutchison, *Chinese Myths and Legends*, p. 10.

Chapter Two: Legendary Stories of Love and Lovers

12. Quoted in *China Daily* (Beijing), "Classic Loves Stories from China," March 15, 2011. www.chinadaily.com.
13. *China Daily* (Beijing), "Classic Loves Stories from China."
14. Minjie Su, "The Butterfly Lovers: A Classic Chinese Love Story," 2022. Medievalists.net. www.medievalists.net.
15. Shuang Ying Han, "The Story of Niu Lang and Zhi Nu," WorldStories. https://worldstories.org.uk.
16. Han, "The Story of Niu Lang and Zhi Nu."

Chapter Three: Tales of Warriors, Weapons, and War

17. Wu Haiyun, "How Guan Yu Became China's God of War, Wealth, and Everything Else," Sixth Tone, August 12, 2020. www.sixthtone.com.
18. Haiyun, "How Guan Yu Became China's God of War, Wealth, and Everything Else."

19. Mark Cartwright, "Ancient Chinese Warfare," *World History Encyclopedia*, November 7, 2017. www.worldhistory.org.
20. Duane and Hutchison, *Chinese Myths and Legends*, pp. 36–37.
21. Duane and Hutchison, *Chinese Myths and Legends*, p. 37.
22. Duane and Hutchison, *Chinese Myths and Legends*, pp. 38, 41.
23. Quoted in Han H. Frankel, *The Flowering Plum and the Palace Lady: Interpretations of Chinese Poetry*. New Haven, CT: Yale University Press, 1976, pp. 68–72.
24. Quoted in Frankel, *The Flowering Plum and the Palace Lady,* p. 70.
25. Quoted in Frankel, *The Flowering Plum and the Palace Lad,* p. 71.

Chapter Four: A Proud Legacy of Mythical Heroes
26. Duane and Hutchison, *Chinese Myths and Legends*, pp. 52–53.
27. Birch, *Tales from China*, p. 11.
28. Birrell, *Chinese Myths*, p. 38.
29. Sanders, *Dragons, Gods, and Spirits from Chinese Mythology*, p. 35.
30. Song Xinyi, "Mu Guiying," *Shanghai Daily* (Shanghai, China), October 22, 2017. https://archive.shine.cn.

Chapter Five: China's Mythical Animals and Monsters
31. Birch, *Tales from China*, pp. 17–18.
32. Ken Liu, "5 Chinese Mythological Creatures That Need to Appear in More SF/F," *B&N Reads* (blog), Barnes & Noble, April 12, 2016. www.barnesandnoble.com.
33. Liu, "5 Chinese Mythological Creatures That Need to Appear in More SF/F."
34. Sara Lynn Hua, "5 Chinese Ghosts That Are Absolutely Terrifying," *TutorMing China Expats & Culture Blog*, October 31, 2016. http://blog.tutorming.com.
35. Hua, "5 Chinese Ghosts That Are Absolutely Terrifying."
36. Hua, "5 Chinese Ghosts That Are Absolutely Terrifying."

HIERARCHY OF ANCIENT CHINA'S BEST-KNOWN GODS

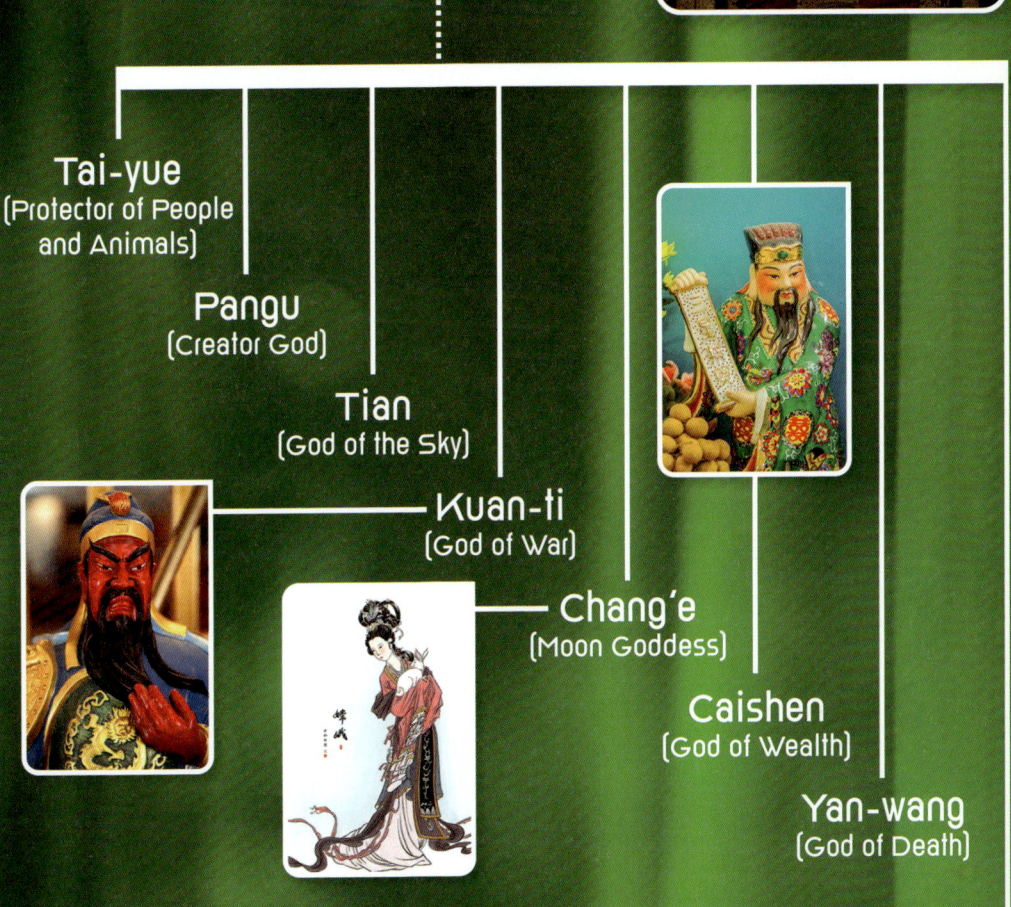

Wang-mu + Jade Emperor

Tai-yue (Protector of People and Animals)

Pangu (Creator God)

Tian (God of the Sky)

Kuan-ti (God of War)

Chang'e (Moon Goddess)

Caishen (God of Wealth)

Yan-wang (God of Death)

Dragons

Yinglong (Dragon King)

Yellow Dragon*

Pearl Dragon*

Black Dragon*

Long Dragon*

*From the tale "The Four Dragons"

59

FOR FURTHER RESEARCH

Books

Tammy Gagne, *Chinese Gods, Heroes, and Mythology*. Minneapolis, MN: ABDO, 2019.

Frederick H. Martins and Richard Wilhelm, *Chinese Fairy Tales and Legends*. Sydney, Australia: Bloomsbury China, 2019.

Aaron Shepard, *The Monkey King: A Superhero Tale of China*. Bellingham, WA: Skyhook, 2019.

Jiankun Sun, *Fantastic Creatures of the Mountains and Seas: A Chinese Classic*. New York: Arcade, 2021.

Mingmet Yip, *Chinese Children's Favorite Stories*. Tokyo, Japan: Tuttle, 2020.

Internet Sources

Sauget Aghikari, "Top 10 Astonishing Ancient Chinese Mythology Stories," Ancient History Lists, November 20, 2019. www.ancienthistorylists.com.

China Culture.org, "Chinese Myth of the Creation of the World and Mankind," December 30, 2019. http://en.chinaculture.org.

Ducksters, "Ancient China: Mythology," 2022. www.ducksters.com.

Ducksters, "Ancient China: Religion," 2022. www.ducksters.com.

Emily Mark, "Ghosts in Ancient China," *World History Encyclopedia*, April 20, 2016. www.ancient.eu.

Edward T.C. Werner, "Myths and Legends of China: Fox Legends," Internet Sacred Text Archive. www.sacred-texts.com.

Shuang Ying Han, "The Story of Niu Lang and Zhi Nu," WorldStories. https://worldstories.org.uk.

Ced Yong, "108 Chinese Mythological Gods and Characters to Know About," Owlcation, April 16, 2022. https://owlcation.com.

Websites

Ancient Chinese Stories, Fables, and Legends for Kids, Ancient China for Kids and Teachers
https://china.mrdonn.org/stories.html
This entertaining site, geared for young readers, features dozens of links, each leading to a short rendition of a common ancient Chinese myth.

Dragons, Qilin, Phoenix and Other Mythical Beasts, Chinasage
www.chinasage.info/dragons.htm
An informative and entertaining site that provides many links to various aspects of Chinese legends, tales, and aspects of culture, both ancient and modern.

The Gods of Chinese Mythology, Godchecker
www.godchecker.com/chinese-mythology
Conceived by the late modern mythologist Chas Saunders, this informational site explains the best-known ancient Chinese gods in a well-designed, eye-catching format.

INDEX